Heidi's Book of Poetry

By

Stephen Cohen

Badman Publishing

Heidi's Book of Poetry

ISBN 979-8-89860-853-8

This book of poetry is from a fictional character call Heidi. She is one of three main protagonists from the *Blue Ring Assassins* book series. As part of her character development in her down time she would right poetry, some of which are included in the books.

The three girls became very close, Heidi took great pleasure from the company of Hannah and Petra, listening to their stories of days gone by.

These poem's, follow Heidi's life as she struggled through some difficult times during WWII. Each poem depicting a certain timeline starting with the onset of war, ending with her demise.

Dedicated to Heidi, your love and bravery, will be forever in our hearts.

Table of Contents

World at War
Snatched
Brothel Nights
A Lost Reflection
Who Am I
Women United
Petra
Hannah
Apple Orchard
Joy and Fun
Her Younger Days
Beloved Auntie
Bombs Are No Delight
Deaths Door
Devil Within
Training
Agents
Copper Coloured Days
Angel of Death
London's Calling
Poison
Perfect Moments
Dangerous Times
Needless Deaths
Lost Souls
Entwined Hearts
Paris – Eiffel Tower
Colosseum
London Blitz
Morning Chorus
When Love Dies
Bravery
Sanctuary
Snowy Mountains
Switzerland
Mountain Breeze
Passing
Memories of Me
The Aftermath of War

World At War

In nineteen thirty-nine, a world at war,
the Second World War, a brutal score.
Axis powers rose, their evil spread,
Hitler, Mussolini, the world in dread.

Blitzkrieg in Europe, blitz on Britain's shores,
the Luftwaffe's reign, the world abhors.

Allies unite, a common goal in sight,
to rid the world of tyranny's blight.

The brave soldiers, heroes all,
their sacrifice, we must recall.
The lessons learned, the price of hate,
may we never again succumb to fate.

World War Two, a dark chapter of history,
but from its ashes, we strive for peace and unity.

Snatched

Snatched from the streets of Berlin,
a tale of loss and sorrow begin.
in the shadows of the night,
a soul disappears out of sight.

A city once vibrant, now hushed,
as memories of a loved one crushed.
The echoes of footsteps fade,
in the darkness, a heart betrayed.

Lost in the maze of city lights,
hope flickers in the cold nights.
Prayers whispered in the wind,
for the one who was snatched, sinned.

Berlin, a city of mystery and pain,
where the streets whisper a haunting refrain.
A life taken without warning,
leaving behind souls mourning.

In the silence of the night,
the truth remains out of sight.
But in the hearts of those left behind,
a memory of a love, that will always bind.

Brothel Nights

Sweet smelling rooms start the day,
soon consumed, by tobacco and essence of man,
body shaking rhythms are assured,
through the doors and the walls,
no point in wishing for nights end,
for tomorrow, we do it all again.

A lost reflection

The mirror has long stopped reflecting self.
Instead, the person I see is just a shell,
void of love, consumed by hatred.
Many people miss loved ones…

Me…I miss myself; the old me, before been
turned into this…monster thirsting for vengeance.
My eyes open a window to a soul that pretends,
strength on the outside but cries for help within me.

I might have escaped death, but I remain trapped by
the past that moulded me.

The world is cruel to a woman's heart.

War has stained the earth with blood, but no cries are heard
for those abused by the hands of narcissistic men.
Nights still haunt me with images of torture and
molestation.

Memories bombard me as I remain stagnant before the
mirror,
lost in gaze at the person staring right back at me…and she
smiles.

Not happily, but with insanity. Her soul is lost to the dark
sides of war,
but finds purpose in bringing retribution to those
responsible,
for what she's become…

Who am I?

Has the world and I, both under threat,
dragged to our feet, to the street and
A choking threat.
No more mellowed heart,
but charge with rage.

If I were a bird, then behold my wings,
no longer trapped by a cage,
They spread and I fly
in this, a world of espionage.

My ears are often deafened
with screams and shots.
The air reeking of stained blood
and death.

Who am I really?
They call me, Heidi
Yielder of death and tragedy.
Rendered to a feud,
that now defines me.

Nay! Not lending my hands to rip
at your heart.
Beware of the blood rush in my veins,
it washes through me like seething waves.

Above me a whirlpool of charcoal clouds,
one day, my heart will smile again.
My eyes no longer filled with pain
I will, find myself, once again.

For now, my name will remain, Heidi.

Women United

Nobody wins in war, no matter the victor,
for every drop of blood that spills, is, humanity's loss.

But war holds many truths, some stifled from existence,
but remains truth nonetheless.
War is largely, of men's honour and bravery,
but women's role will show and last.

Oppressed and ill-treated due to gender bias,
women bare the weight of sexist agendas,
intent on diminishing their worth in the field.
The inner strength to fight for a country
that yields on male dominancy,
holding us in society's hierarchy.

Bring forth the wealth of women.
Let their strengths shine through,
While still sacrificing, some giving their lives in battle.
Raising a nation, while still fighting for one.

Patriotism holds no colour, race, nor gender,
but is a reflection of the hearts and souls of those
who fight for it.

We fight against tyranny; we stand to be counted!

Petra

In shadows she moves, graceful and swift
Petra, the beautiful assassin, her presence a gift.
With eyes like daggers, she sees through the night
a deadly beauty, a formidable sight.

Her steps are silent, her movements like a dance,
each kill executed with deadly precision, by chance.
Her beauty a mask, a facade she wears,
as she navigates through the dangers and snares

A whisper in the wind, a shadow in the dark
Petra, strikes fear in the hearts of her mark.
But behind the cold steel, the lethal intent
lies a soul tormented, a life misspent.

For she is not just a killer, a weapon for hire,
but a woman haunted by her burning desire.
To right the wrongs, to seek justice and truth,
in a world where darkness thrives, in her ruthless pursuit.

Petra, the beautiful assassin, a tale untold
of a woman with a heart, of secrets she holds.
In the silence of the night, in the depths of her soul,
lies a story of love and loss, of a past she can't control.

Hannah

In a world of chaos and strife,
there shines a beauty, pure and rife.
Hannah, with her graceful eyes,
like stars that light up, darkened skies.

Her laughter, like a melody,
brings warmth and joy to all who see.
Her kindness, like a gentle breeze,
calms the storms and sets hearts at ease.

In her presence, all things bloom,
as if touched by a magic broom.
Her spirit, bright and full of grace,
illuminates the darkest space.

Oh Hannah, with your beauty rare,
a gift to all who breathe the air.
May your light forever shine,
and may your heart be always kind.

Hannah

Apple Orchard

Saplings grace the grassy land,
planted by hardened hands.
Cared for by tender hearts,
saplings grow to hardened bark.

The first few years pass by
tendering young trees.
Until the first blooming begins,
bringing with it emerging fruit.

Shadows extend with passing years,
branches stretching to the skies.
Bees are busy buzzing by
laying new pollen, bringing life.

Summer sun growing spheres,
reds and greens of coloured delights.
Pies and ciders tasty sugar treats,
apple orchard, rejoice, in what it brings.

Joy and Fun

Cent of blossom fills the air,
morning mist burnt off by the sun,
days full of joy and fun.

She plays with her friend,
boundless days of fun,
enjoying life bumble-bees come.

She watches them working hard,
buzzing between the blossom,
pollination now begun.

They play here every day,
running, ducking under leaves,
branches stretching to the skies.

For weeks they watch,
apples form and ripen in the sun,
once they fall harvest has begun.

Returning home, pockets full,
in hope of baking with her mum,
apple pie brings joy and fun.

Her Younger Days

Sun always shinning,
no shadow over her,
no screaming in her ears,
no blood-stained tears,
she lays and rests,
on her father's lap,
he wraps his arms around,
feeling safe and relaxed.

He carries her off to bed,
tucks her in, kisses her forehead,
she snuggles down and drifts to sleep,
her dreams are full of bliss,
sun blazing through her window,
a new day begins,
chores to be done, she helps her mum,
she can't wait for the fun, to begin.

Beloved Auntie

Beloved auntie, with a heart so kind,
forever in my memories, I'll find.
Your warm embrace, your gentle touch,
your wisdom guiding me so much.

You filled my days with laughter and love,
a shining light from up above.
In times of joy and times of sorrow,
you were there, today and tomorrow.

Your words of wisdom, so pure and true,
guiding me in all that I do.
You showed me how to be strong and brave,
your love and support, forever I'll crave.

Beloved auntie, you mean the world to me,
in my heart, you'll always be.
Forever grateful for all to see,
my precious auntie.

Bombs Are No Delight

Humming engines fill the skies,
the sirens wail, the warning dies,
the planes fly over,
bleeding out payloads, screeching down,
despondent faces search the skies.

Running for cover, where to hide,
targets found, a booming sound,
rubble falling, shattering glass,
bringing destruction and on mass,
in my heart, survive the blast.

Dust and smoke fill my lungs,
my body crushing, from the boom,
trying to listen, to frightening sounds,
muffled ears, hums abound,
falling wreckage hits the ground.

Deaths Door

The fear of dying grips my soul,
a darkness lurking, taking hold.
I long to live, to breathe, to be,
but death's cold hand beckons me.

The fear of dying, a constant foe,
whispers of mortality, where I go.
I pray for peace, for strength, for grace,
to keep the fear at bay, in its place.

But still it lingers, a shadow dark,
creeping through my thoughts, leaving its mark.
I try to push it away, to ignore,
but the fear of dying knocks at my door.

I know one day, my time will come,
to face the unknown, the beat of the drum.
But until then, I'll fight the fear,
and live my life, without a tear.

Devil within

Blood lay seeping into the land and
filtered away by the sea.
This blood, a reflection of humanity,
tarnished lands near and far.
This war demands a lot from thee,
all in the name, to be free.

The time has come to make a stand,
against the horrors of tyranny.
By land, by air and sea
We will stand together in harmony,
we are the fighter's you don't see,
fighting together for victory.

From a distance we draw you in,
but be aware, of the devil within.
We let you touch our soft silk skin,
from here your death will begin.
Your last breath drawn, your eyes go dim,
you've been touch by beauty and the devil within.

Training

In shadows deep, they learn to creep,
through covert missions, secrets to keep.
A life of danger, a code to live by,
a secret agent, trained to spy.

Disguises worn, identities shed,
In the world of espionage, where trust is dead.
They learn to fight, to blend and to deceive,
for in this world, nothing is as it seems.

Hand to hand combat, weapons trained,
in the art of war, they are well versed and ingrained.
Mental fortitude, sharp as a blade,
their training solid, their loyalty never swayed.

Silent steps, quick reflexes,
in the life of a spy, there are no excesses.
A life on the edge, a constant test,
but for their country, they give their best.

So here's to the secret agents in the dark,
the unsung heroes, who leave their mark.
In the shadows they work, silent and unseen,
forever loyal, forever keen.

Agents

Divided by love and hate,
for a country that swells with tyranny.

Air tainted with unfamiliar smells,
gun powder and death on the field's dwell.
Into the ground go wooden stakes and,
wire, does another line make.

Shoulder to shoulder on both sides,
do soldiers fight with all their might.
But in the shadows are lurking spies,
agents of death, not shining bright.

Their minds are their tools, but don't be fooled,
trickery and treachery are their game.
Their hidden weapons will be your doom.
they creep in shadows or in plain sight.

Carriers of death without a doubt!

Coppered Coloured Days

My life is an old copper bath,
old and no longer used,
not yet rusted but corroding with time,
waiting for someone to polish me,
back to that free moment in time,
we go through life feeling the pain,
of those long passed, memories remain.
our skin grows old, but in our eyes,
the pain doesn't fade.
It's just copper coloured,
over time.

Angle of death

Angel of death,
as she, is known,
on swift wings,
we are thrown,
into a world, of unknown.

Hearts once swollen,
with love and joy,
are turned to stone,
deadly hands, we are shown.

With iron fist,
she does rule,
no method to madness,
brutality is her tool.

London's Calling

London's calling, a voice so clear,
whispers of history, we hold dear,
the city's heartbeat, pulsing strong,
a melody in every street, every song.

From the Thames to Big Ben's chime,
London's charm, oh so divine,
tales of kings and queens untold,
in every stone, in every stronghold.

The bustling markets, the bustling crowds,
the city alive, it speaks so loud,
from the dusty blitz, it reaches out,
learn new skills, let them unfold.

So heed the call, come take a chance,
in London's embrace, let your spirit dance,
for in this city, you'll find your place,
London's calling, future untold.

Poison

Hidden in the shadows, a deadly brew,
lurking in the darkness, waiting for you,
a silent killer, creeping near,
beware the poison, do not fear.

Its venomous touch, a vicious sting,
like a serpent's bite, it does its thing.
Slow and insidious, it spreads its pain,
leaving behind a trail of disdain.

Invisible yet potent, it takes its toll,
a lethal potion that steals the soul.
A treacherous elixir, a toxic blend,
beware the poison, do not descend.

So guard your heart, your mind, your soul,
against the poison's deadly role.
For once it takes hold, it's hard to break free,
from the grip of this sinister enemy.

So be vigilant, be wary, be wise,
and keep the poison at bay, in disguise.
For in this world, where darkness reigns,
the poison lingers, waiting to claim.

Perfect Moments

Not defined, perfect moments,
lost in time, perfect moments,
where do you hide.

In the reaches of my mind,
doors are closed, eyes open wide,
as I journey through this time.

Life determined by my mind,
it's my place, it's my mind,
find it hard to close my eyes.

Those darkened times called night,
things just rattle in my mind,
life undetermined, time goes by.

Perfect moments, where do you hide.

Dangerous Times

Bags packed once again, the journey starts,
at the station, coal fires burning,
carrying that familiar soot smell,
on the platforms, porters yell,
trains destination, could be hell.

Papers checked by men in black,
but it's the ones you don't see,
suited, wearing hats,
searching crowds for their pray,
no quarter given, your taken away.

Today's news in hand,
gazing down on a page,
not wanting to engage their rage,
longing for a sounding whistle,
it's time to leave, and swallow.

Needless Deaths

Muffled gun shots fill the air,
the scream of bombs everywhere,
day and night we hear the cries,
hearts are pounding, eyes are glazed,
I hope this day, is not my end.

Endless days are all the same,
family and friends no longer remain,
millions are lost every year,
not just those on the fields,
but those in homes, the fear is real.

Bodies scattered on streets and fields,
the stench of death is all it yields,
crying echoes in the air,
feeling of loss and despair,
you try to shake, them awake,
to no end, it is their fate.

Lost Souls

The seasons pass, a year has gone,
endless life's mourning loss,
on swift wings death can come,
silence stricken with their screams.

Rivers of blood flow endlessly,
screaming men, their pain revealed,
dust and smoke rise like a wall,
those who can, try to crawl.

There is so many, can't save them all,
troubled faces standing tall,
for those laying on the floor,
tomorrow may be never more.

Nightmares haunt my mind and soul,
there is no god, or so I'm told,
for if there was, he would take hold,
and bring an end to losing souls.

Entwined Hearts

He was a soldier, brave and true,
she was a nurse, with eyes of blue.
Their love blossomed in the midst of chaos,
but war as a way of stealing and loss.

Dreams of a future together shattered,
as the world around them crumbled and scattered.
He fought for his country, she cared for the wounded,
but their love was tested and severely wounded.

But as the war raged on, their love slowly died,
broken dreams of a future they once eyed.
He was called away to fight in a distant land,
leaving her behind with a heavy heart and empty hand.

She waited for his return, with hope in her soul,
but deep down she knew, it was taking a toll.
Years passed by, and still, he did not come back,
leaving her with a heart that felt like a crack.

Their love story ended in tragedy and pain,
as she whispered his name in the pouring rain.
In the heart of Italy, where memories remain,
their broken dreams of love, forever stained.

Paris – Eiffel Tower

Standing proud in the city of light,
a tower of lattice iron, reaches for the sky,
enduring the passing of time,
unbowed, this beacon of light.

Parisian and visitors alike,
marvel at its artistry and the love that might.
A breathtaking, wondrous symbol,
of engineering might.

Named after the vision of a man,
Eiffel, where romance blooms, dreams take flight,
under the Eiffel Towers watchful sight,
lovers steal a kiss by moon light.

Views at the top are simply divine,
below a silver line, the Seine,
reflects back, a moment captured in time,
scraping at the depths of hearts and minds.

Paris, you city of light, with your iconic star,
a shimmering spectacle you do share,
in shadows of the tower,
we find solace there.

Colosseum

In Rome stands a marvel ancient and grand,
the Colosseum, a world wonder, in the heart of the land,
with history etched in every stone,
echoes of gladiators' battles still shown.

Emperors, warriors, and crowds did fill,
the great amphitheatre, a testament to skill,
of architects and builders from eras past,
whose legacy in stone forever cast.

The blood and sweat of battles fought,
the cheers and jeers, the emotions sought,
in this arena of tales untold,
where history and glory unfold.

Oh Rome, your Colosseum stands proud,
a symbol of a bygone age, unbowed,
reminding us of the power and might,
of a city that once ruled with all its might..

London – The Blitz

The Blitz, they called it, a terror from above,
destroying homes, tearing cities of love.

Children huddled in shelters, trembling with fear,
as the roar of the planes grew ever near.

Families torn apart, by the bombs' cruel might,
in the black of night, they fought for their right.

To live in peace, to see another dawn,
in the face of destruction, they carried on.

Through the rubble and ruin, they held their heads high,
their spirit unbroken, reaching for the sky.

Courage and solidarity, in the face of despair,
a nation united, in a fight against terror.

The London Blitz, a chapter in history's book,
where ordinary people, through hardship, took.

Their place in the annals of bravery and strength,
a testament to the human spirit's length.

So let us remember, those who gave their all,
in the face of adversity, answering the call.

To stand firm in the storm, to never retreat,
for their sacrifice, our gratitude complete.

Fields of Fire

Soldiers pushing on,
hails of bullets all around,
we will never forget those lost,
lost in the fields of fire.

For some the sun will set,
their memory lives on,
every position defended,
every bullet sent, every inch of ground.

Brothers in arms,
nothing more to give,
those that remain,
fighting fearlessly,
the fear raging within.

On the field of fire,
where some many fall,
you'll never be forgotten,
from dusk till dawn,
we will remember your sacrifice.

Morning Chorus

The whistles of gunshots, bring the night alive.
The fear it brings with it, hope fills your mind,
will I make it thought the night?
Eyes gaze in to the darkness, the only light, like fire flies,
bullets flying in the night.

Jack frost visits the evening plight,
brings with him a chill, piercing to the bone.
Winter is upon us, in the trenches, men are cold,
but once the cockcrow starts a calling,
a robin joins the lines, with morning chorus.

Death dawns on ardent hearts,
yes, for some, this will be their last, first light.

When Love Dies

When love dies, it's like a tree losing its leaves,
slowly withering away, until nothing but memories it
leaves.
It's like a flame slowly fading, losing its heat,
leaving a cold emptiness, where once there was a sweet
retreat.

The joy and laughter that once filled the air,
now replaced with silence and despair.
The tender touch that used to ignite a fire,
now feels like a distant memory, lost in the mire.

The promises made with such sincerity,
now shattered like fragile glass, no longer in clarity.
The trust once so strong, now fragile and weak,
like a dam breaking apart, unable to speak.

When love dies, it's a pain that cuts deep,
Leaving scars that are hard to heal and steep.
The dreams once shared, now shattered and broken,
Leaving behind a heart that feels forsaken.

But even in the darkness of love's demise,
there is hope for new beginnings to arise.
For love may die, but it can also be reborn,
in a stronger form, weathered and worn.

So mourn the loss, grieve the pain,
but know that love can rise again.
For when love dies, it's not the end,
but a new chapter waiting to be penned.

Bravery

In the days of World War II,
a battle raged, both old and new.
Countries clashed in brutal strife,
fathers and sons gave up their life's.

Tanks rolled across the battlefield,
the sound of gunfire never yield.
Soldiers fought with all their might,
through the day and into the night.

In the midst of chaos and despair,
courageous hearts were everywhere.
Women stepped into the fray,
aiding in the fight, come what may.

Families torn apart by war,
praying for loved ones ajar.
In the darkest hour, a beacon of hope,
united we stood, we could cope.

Allies joined in solidarity,
to defeat the Axis mentality.
Freedom was the prize we sought,
with every battle bravely fought.

Sanctuary

This Swiss home of sanctuary, mountains tall,
where peace and beauty overlap in awe,
the air is crisp, the landscape pure and grand,
a refuge from the chaos of the land.

Embrace the quietude, the gentle breeze,
among the rolling hills and snowy trees,
the sound of cowbells in the meadows ring,
a tranquil melody that softly sings.

This Swiss home of sanctuary, find solace,
in nature's arms, where troubles are erased,
a haven where the heart can find its rest,
and all the world's worries are suppressed.

So let us cherish this enchanted land,
where mountains meet the sky and valleys stand,
this Swiss home of sanctuary, may we stay,
and let our souls be free in every way.

Snowy Mountains

Switzerland's snowy mountains majestic and grand,
a winter wonderland in a far-off land.
the peaks stretch high into the sky,
a sight that will make you sigh.

The snow glistens under the sun's bright light,
a truly breathtaking sight.
the air is crisp and cold,
but the beauty of these mountains never gets old.

Skiing down the slopes with ease,
the feeling of freedom, the feeling of peace.
the Swiss Alps call to those who seek,
a thrill, an adventure, a mountain peak.

So if you ever find yourself in Switzerland's snowy
mountains,
take a moment to appreciate their beauty, their fountains.
for nature's wonders are all around,
in these snowy mountains, where peace is found.

Switzerland

Oh Switzerland with your mountains high,
your beauty takes my breath away,
green valleys and lakes that lie,
bathed in the sun's golden ray.

Your people strong and peaceful,
with hearts as pure as snow,
in every town and bustling city,
a sense of harmony doth flow.

The Swiss watches ticking away,
in precision and perfection,
reflecting a nation's pride,
in craftsmanship and dedication.

From Zurich to Geneva's shores,
your beauty knows no bounds,
a paradise for all who seek,
in Switzerland, true bliss is found.

So here's to you, Switzerland,
land of beauty and grace,
may your flag forever fly,
in this peaceful, picturesque place.

Mountain Breeze

Mountain breeze through my hair,
whispers of freedom in the air.
A symphony of nature's song,
as I stand where I belong.

The cool touch of the wind,
leaves a sense of calm within.
Majestic peaks reach for the sky,
I feel small, yet so alive.

The scent of pine fills my soul,
as I embrace the mountains whole.
In this moment, I am free,
with the mountain breeze, just me.

Passing

Do not grieve my passing,
memories everlasting.

Do not weep for me,
for in your heart, I rest.

Steady your trembling
heart and hands, give comfort to those
in greater need.

Do not seek out the darkness
and company of gathering dust to weep.
Rejoice in my life, for I, have only, returned
from whence I came.

Heidi

Age 21

Born
Dresden 1920

Died January 1944

Heidi

Memories Of Me

One day years from now,
you will remember me,
long gone laying in the ground,
but your memories of me, riding high,
music playing bring memories alive,
volume up, playing high,
reminiscing of days gone by,
you will remember me,

In those days, those days gone by,

Laying now in darkness,
my essence still remains,
in your memories,
my life resides.

The Aftermath of War

In the heart of battle, in the heat of war,
they stood as one, against the enemy's roar.
The soldiers fought on, with courage and might,
in the darkness of night, in the broad daylight.

Their faces grim, their eyes filled with dread,
but they forged ahead, with hearts pure and red.
In the midst of chaos, they held their line,
with bravery and honour, they continued to shine.

Each step they took, a sacrifice made,
for freedom and peace, they were unafraid.
Through fields of death, they marched on,
with hope in their hearts, for a brighter dawn.

They gave their all, they gave their best,
in WWII, they faced the ultimate test.
They fought for their country, they fought for their kin,
they fought for a world free from tyranny's sin.
and though many fell, and many were lost,
their memory lives on, at such a great cost.

So let us remember, let us never forget,
the heroes of WAR, whose sacrifice we can't regret.
For they gave their last, they gave it all,
in defence of freedom, they stood tall.